by Martin G. Plainfield
illustrated by Matthew Baek

SCHOOL PUBLISHERS

Printed in China

ISBN 10: 0-15-350974-0
ISBN 13: 978-0-15-350974-2

Ordering Options
ISBN 10: 0-15-350601-6 (Grade 4 On-Level Collection)
ISBN 13: 978-0-15-350601-7 (Grade 4 On-Level Collection)
ISBN 10: 0-15-357927-7 (package of 5)
ISBN 13: 978-0-15-357927-1 (package of 5)

4 5 6 7 8 9 10 0940 12 11 10 09

Kayla was feeling very discouraged because
she was stuck spending her Saturday afternoon
picking weeds from the garden. Kayla and her
mother, father, and younger brother lived in
a small house in the country. The garden was
behind her family's house. A farmer had
abandoned the field long ago. Now the town
owned it, and everyone in the area shared the
garden. They also shared the chores, and it was
her family's turn to do the weeding.

"Can I stop now, Mom?" Kayla asked, as she pushed up her hat and wiped her forehead.

"You don't want the weeds to ruin the vegetables now, do you, dear?" her mother replied. To Kayla, pulling weeds was complete and total drudgery.

Despite disliking the task, though, she kept doing it. She carefully separated the weeds from the plants, plucked the weeds from the soil, and threw them into an old bushel basket. As they worked, Kayla noticed that the sky was getting cloudy. She welcomed the break from the hot sun.

A half hour passed, and the sky had become much darker than before. It was obvious to Kayla that a storm was on the way, but her mother didn't seem to be worried about it. She was happy to be tending to the garden, wearing her wide-brimmed hat, sunglasses, and gardening gloves.

"Look how dark the sky is getting—I think a tornado is coming," Kayla said.

"Nonsense," her mother scoffed, looking up at the sky. "It looks like a typical summer storm. The air gets heated all day and produces a few thunderstorms later in the afternoon. We don't have anything to worry about."

Before long, a light rain began to fall, and the sky grew even darker. Then the rain started to come down harder. Kayla's mother finally stopped and picked up the bushel basket. "All right, Kayla," she said, "your work is through for the day, thanks to this rain."

They turned to walk back to the house. Then they heard a loud clap of thunder, and they ran the rest of the way. Inside the safety of the house, Kayla said, "I've never seen the sky so dark. There must be a tornado coming."

"Let's not get carried away because of a little thunderstorm," her mother said skeptically.

It was darker than ever now, and it looked slightly green outside. Bright blasts of lightning lit up the sky, and more thunder exploded. Kayla's father and brother were on a canoe trip together. She wished that they were home. Then Kayla glanced out the window and saw a tall, twisting funnel-shaped cloud far in the distance. "Mom, look!" Kayla yelled. Her mother ran to the window and looked out. At the same time, they heard the town's tornado siren go off.

"Now that's a tornado all right!" Kayla's mom said, and immediately she and Kayla plunged into the basement.

In the basement, Kayla's mother pulled out a flashlight, candles, matches, and a small radio from their emergency kit. Then they went to a corner away from the basement windows. They turned on the radio and listened as the announcer said that there had been a tornado sighted in their county.

Kayla and her mother crawled under the heavy workbench and got into a crouched position for greater safety. They could hear the tornado roaring closer. "Don't worry, we're safe down here," said Kayla's mother.

As Kayla and her mother were crouched under the workbench, the tornado roared toward the house. The noise grew louder and louder until it sounded like a freight train was coming. They could hear loud thumps and bangs, and Kayla imagined things flying around and trees coming down in the wind.

Suddenly, Kayla felt the whole house rattle and shake. She screamed when some plaster from the ceiling fell. Kayla and her mother covered their heads, but they were safe under the workbench. The tornado's roar was at its loudest. Kayla felt like a statue, frozen with fear.

"Mom!" she yelled.

"Hang in there!" answered her mother.

After another frightening minute, the noise lessened, and the shaking stopped. "I think it's moving away from us now," said Kayla's mother, still crouching and covering her head.

They stayed in the basement, waiting for the all-clear siren to sound. They listened to the radio some more, and the reports said that the tornado was now long past them. Then they heard the all-clear siren and knew it was safe to come out.

"We survived, baby," her mother said. They hugged for a moment, and then they carefully went upstairs.

When they reached the top of the stairs, they could see the sky and immediately realized that part of their roof had blown off. The big kitchen window was broken, and there was a lot of glass on the floor. Kayla saw many of the family's items strewn about the kitchen, such as papers, cups, and silverware.

Kayla was upset and wanted to cry. It was so sad to see her house like this. Her mother had tears in her eyes, too, as she slowly walked through the wreckage, looking at what had survived the tornado and what hadn't. "Let's check outside," Mom suggested.

They went out the front door. Everything looked altered.

"Look at the Anderson's house!" said Kayla's mother, pointing across the field. Half of their neighbor's house had been knocked over by the storm. The dust hanging in the air made it look like a fire was smoldering.

Kayla and her mother ran over to see if Mrs. Anderson was all right. They found her sitting on her back porch, holding her head in her hands. Kayla and her mother gave Mrs. Anderson a hug and assured her that everything would be fine. They urged Mrs. Anderson to come with them.

They were shocked to see the tornado's destruction: trees were down all over the area, and many of the houses were damaged. There were papers, wood, clothing, and broken furniture scattered everywhere. It was very treacherous just walking around.

"You see," said Kayla's mother pointing to the field, "the tornado came right through here in a straight line and wiped out everything in its path."

They heard sirens in the background. "It could have been a lot worse. We're all okay," my mother said to Mrs. Anderson.

"Mom, let's go check on the garden," Kayla said. She and her mother walked to the field and saw that most of the plants were not harmed.

"The roots held them in," said Kayla's mother. As they looked at the tomato and corn plants, the sun came back out, and it brightened up. Kayla turned to her mother.

"The plants survived the storm just like we did, Mom," she said.

"That's right, dear, we made it through," said her mother. "Let's go call Dad and make sure he knows we're all right!"

"Good idea, Mom," answered Kayla. "You know, a boring Saturday pulling weeds doesn't sound so bad at all right now."

Think Critically

1. Why wasn't Kayla's mother concerned about the approaching storm?

2. How would you describe Kayla?

3. How could Kayla and her mother tell that the tornado was past them?

4. What word means almost the same thing as *treacherous* does on page 13?

5. Do you think this story could be true? Why or why not?

 Science

Write a Paragraph Look up information about tornadoes. Then write a paragraph that explains how they are formed and where they are most likely to happen.

School-Home Connection Tell a family member about this story. Then have a discussion about dangerous weather situations that family members have experienced.

Word Count: 1,167